THE FEMALE ACADEMY

CAST LIST
Two Grave Matrons belonging to the Female Academy
Two or three Antient Ladies
Two or three Citizens Wives
A Company of young Gentlemen and others.

ACT I

SCENE I

Enter **TWO ANTIENT LADIES**.

FIRST LADY
If you would have your Daughter virtuously and wisely educated, you must put her into the Female Academy.

SECOND LADY
The Female Academy, what is that?

FIRST LADY
Why a House, wherein a company of young Ladies are instructed by old Matrons; as to speak wittily and rationally, and to behave themselves handsomly, and to live virtuously.

SECOND LADY

Do any men come amongst them?

FIRST LADY
O no; only there is a large open Grate, where on the out-side men stand, which come to hear and see them; but no men enter into the Academy, nor women, but those that are put in for Education; for they have another large open Grate at the other end of the Room they discourse in; where on the out-side of that Grate stand women that come to hear them discourse.

SECOND LADY
I will put my Daughter therein to be instructed.

FIRST LADY

If your Daughter were not of honourable Birth, they would not receive her, for they take in none but those of antient Descent, as also rich, for it is a place of charges.

SECOND LADY
Why then they will not refuse my Daughter, for she is both honourably born, and also rich.

[Exeunt.

SCENE II

Enter a Company of **YOUNG LADIES**, and with them **TWO GRAVE MATRONS**; where through the Hanging a company of **MEN** look on them, as through a Grate

FIRST MATRON
Come Lady, 'tis your turn this day to take the Chair.

[All sit, and she that speaks sits in an adorned Chair.

LADY SPEAKER
Deliver your Theam.

FIRST MATROD
You speak Lady like a Robber, when he sayes deliver your Purse; but you must say propound your Team.

LADY SPEAKER
Why then propound your Theam.

FIRST MATRON
I present to your opinion, whether women are capable to have as much Wit or Wisdome as men.

LADY SPEAKER
First, I must define what Wit and Wisdome are: as for Wit, it is the Daughter of Nature, and Wisdome is a Son of the Gods: this Daughter of Nature, the Lady Wit, is very beautiful, and for the most part her

The Female Academy by Margaret Cavendish

Margaret Lucas Cavendish, Duchess of Newcastle-upon-Tyne was born in 1623 in Colchester, Essex into a family of comfortable means.

As the youngest of eight children she spent much time with her siblings. Margaret had no formal education but she did have access to scholarly libraries and tutors, although she later said the children paid little attention to the tutors, who were there 'rather for formality than benefit'.

From an early age Margaret was already assembling her thoughts for future works despite the then conditions of society that women did not partake in public authorship. For England it was also a time of Civil War. The Royalists were being pushed back and Parliamentary forces were in the ascendancy.

Despite these obvious dangers, when Queen Henrietta Maria was in Oxford, Margaret asked her mother for permission to become one of her Ladies-in-waiting. She was accepted and, in 1644, accompanied the Queen into exile in France. This took her away from her family for the first time.

Despite living at the Court of the young King Louis XIV, life for the young Margaret was not what she expected. She was far from her home and her confidence had been replaced by shyness and difficulties fitting in to the grandeur of her surroundings and the eminence of her company.

Margaret told her mother she wanted to leave the Court. Her mother was adamant that she should stay and not disgrace herself by leaving. She provided additional funds for her to make life easier. Margaret remained. It was now also that she met and married William Cavendish who, at the time, was the Marquis of Newcastle (and later Duke). He was also 30 years her senior and previously married with two children.

As Royalists, a return to life in England was not yet possible. They would remain in exile in Paris, Rotterdam and Antwerp until the restoration of the crown in 1660 although Margaret was able to return for attention to some estate matters.

Along with her husband's brother, Sir Charles Cavendish, she travelled to England after having been told that her husband's estate (taken from him due to his being a royalist) was to be sold and that she, as his wife, would receive some benefit of the sale. She received nothing. She left England to be with her husband again.

The couple were devoted to each other. Margaret wrote that he was the only man she was ever in love with, loving him not for title, wealth or power, but for merit, justice, gratitude, duty, and fidelity. She also relied upon him for support in her career. The marriage provided no children despite efforts made by her physician to overcome her inability to conceive.

Margaret's first book, 'Poems and Fancies', was published in 1653; it was a collection of poems, epistles and prose pieces which explores her philosophical, scientific and aesthetic ideas.

For a woman at this time writing and publishing were avenues they had great difficulty in pursuing. Added to this was Margaret's range of subjects. She wrote across a number of issues including gender, power, manners, scientific method, and philosophy.

She always claimed she had too much time on her hands and was therefore able to indulge her love of writing. As a playwright she produced many works although most are as closet dramas. (This is a play not intended to be performed onstage, but instead read by a solitary reader or perhaps out loud in a small group. For Margaret the rigours of exile, her gender and Cromwell's closing of the theatres mean this was her early vehicle of choice and, despite these handicaps, she became one of the most well-known playwrights in England)

Her utopian romance, 'The Blazing World', (1666) is one of the earliest examples of science fiction. Margaret also published extensively in natural philosophy and early modern science; at least a dozen books.

She was the first woman to attend a meeting at Royal Society of London in 1667 and she criticized and engaged with members and philosophers Thomas Hobbes, René Descartes, and Robert Boyle.

Margaret was always defended against any criticism by her husband and he also contributed to some of her works. She also gives him credit as her writing tutor.

Perhaps a little strangely she said her ambition despite her shyness, was to have everlasting fame. During her career, from the mid 1650's until her death, she was prolific. In recent decades her work has undergone a resurgence of interest propelled mainly by her ground-breaking attitude and accomplishments in those male straitened times.

Margaret Cavendish died on 15th December 1673 and was buried at Westminster Abbey.

Index of Contents

Countenance is very Amiable, and her Speech delightful; in her Acoustrements she is as all other of the Female Sex are, various; as sometimes in plain Garments, and sometimes in glittering Garments; and sometimes she is attired in Garments of as many several Colours as the Rainbow; and she alters in their Fashions, as often as in their Substances or Trimmings: as for her humour, it is according to the nature of her Sex, which is as various and changing as her Acoustrements; for that sometimes she is merry and jesting, other times pleasing and delightfull; sometimes melancholy, sometimes fantastical, other times spightfull and censorious, and oft times wild and wanton, unless discretion rules and leads her, who keeps her within the bounds and pales of Modesty; also her discourses are various, as sometimes she will flatter grosly, other times she will rail maliciously, and sometimes she will speak so eloquently, and demean her self so elegantly, as to ravish the minds of the beholders and hearers: This Lady Wit hath nine Daughters, very beautifull Ladies, namely the Nine Muses; and every several Muse partakes of every several Humour of the Mother: These nine beautifull Ladies, Natures Grand-children, and Wits Daughters, have vowed single lives, living alwayes in the Court with their Mother, whose Court is a very glorious Palace; for it is composed of Coelestial flame, and Divine Spirits were the Architectures thereof; the Servants and Courtiers of the Lady Wit are Poets, men of all Nations, Qualities, Dignities and Humours; these Courtiers the Poets, make love to the Lady Wits Daughters, the nine Muses, and often receive favours from them; which favours their Servants the Poets braid them into Rimes, and make several works of Verse, then tie them into True Lovers Knots, and then as all Lovers use to do, with their Mistresses favours, vaingloriously shew them to the publick view of the world; for though the Lady Muses will not marry, yet they receive Courtly addresses, and take delight to be wooed aud sued to; the younger sort of Poets are Amorous Lovers; the Grave and more antient Poets are Platonick Lovers, and some are Divine Lovers, and some are Heroick Lovers, and some are Satyrical Lovers, which wooe in a crabbid stile: but to conclude of Wit, there are good Wits which have foolish Judgements; for though Wit and Wisdome are Sisters and Brothers, both the Children of Nature, yet for the most part, the Brother is a meer Fool, and the Sister hath a great wit; but some have Masculine Wits, and Effeminate Judgements, as if their beams were Hermophrica.

The next I am to define is Wisdome, who as I said, is a Son of the Gods: this Wisdome is a person of perfect and upright Shape, of well-composed Features, of a manly Garb, and an assured Countenance, In his speech he is of a readie delivery, and he hath a well-tempered Humour: as for the Acoustrements of his Person, he changes them according to the times and occasions: His constant habitation is in the strong Tower of Honestie, this Tower is built round, without ends or corners, or by places; and it stands upon four Pillars, as Prudence, Fortitude, Justice and Temporance; upon every several Pillar are Letters ingraven, wherein may be read the proper uses, benefits, and advantages of each Pillar: These Pillars of Support, causes this Tower to be inpregnable; for though there are many assaults made against it, as by Riches, which shoots his golden Bullets out of his golden Canons at it, striving to batter it down; and Power brings a mighty Army to assault it, and Danger of Death strives to storm it, and Flattery and Insinuation to undermine it, yet it holds out without any breach therein; for the walls of this Tower, named Honesty, are of a wonderfull strength, for they are as durable as an intire Diamond, not to be dissolved, and as transparant as a Christal, without the least spot, stain, or blemish: In this Tower as I said, lives Wisdom, a most magnificent Lord he is, and is attended numerously and nobly: his chief Favourite is Truth, his chief Counselors are Reason, Understanding, Observation, Experience, and Judgement; his chief Officers are Patience, Industry, and Opportunity; his Domestick Servants are the Appetites, which Servants he rules and governs with great moderation; his Nobility are the Passions, which he peferrs according to their merit; but those that are apt to be Factious, he severely punishes, for he is one that loves peace, and hates brulleries, or any dissention: he is a person of the quickest Sense, for he hath a most piercing sight to foresee dangers, as to avoid them, and can well distinguish the right ways from the wrong; likewise he hath a most cleer hearing, for nothing passes by that concerns him, but the sound gives him an Alarum to stand upon his guard, or a charge to take his advantage; but he hath a silent tongue, for he never speaks but it is to some purpose also he hath a marvelous quick Scent, to smel out a Rebellion or Treason, and he will follow it pace by pace, as Hounds do Hares, and never leaves till he hath hunted it out; also his Touch is very sensible, he soon feels a courtesie or injury, the first he receives gratefully, and feels tenderly, the other he receives strongly, and gripes hard, when he can take fast hold, otherwise he lets it passe or fall, as if his touch were numb'd; he is a person which is so solicited by the weak, sought to by the wronged, flattered by the ambitious, sued to by the distressed; and he often sits in the Court of Errors, to rectifie the disorder therein: sometimes he hath been in great humane Councels, but that is very rare; indeed he is so seldome in great humane Councels, as he is hardly known, for not one among a thousand that did ever see him, much lesse to have any acquaintance with him, for he is reserved, and not company for every one: But there are many that falsly pretend not only to be acquainted with him, but gets false Vizards, and pretend to be Wisdome it self, and the world for the most part is cozened and abused with these Cheats, in not knowing the right & true Wisdom and how should they? when Wisdom it self appears so seldome, as he is a stranger even in Kings Courts and Princes Palaces, and so great a stranger he is in many Courts and Councels, that if by chance he should be there, they thrust him out as a troublesome Guest, and laugh at his advice as foolish, or condemn his Counsel as treacherous: but now I have declared unto you whom Wit and Wisdome are, now I am to give my opinion whether women are capable of their Society; but truly I must tell you it is a difficult question, by reason the several Educations, which are the Ushers that lead humane Creatures to several Societies, for there are Societies of the Ignorant and foolish, as well as of the witty and wise, and several Ushers belonging thereto; and indeed these latter Societies are numerous, and of all sorts; the other are Societies of the most choicest, for though Wit is not an absolute Goddesse, nor humane Wisdome an absolute God, yet they are a degree above other earthly mortals, but Fools are produced from the degrees of Mortality, and Ignorance is the Daughter of Obscurity; the Ushers o these are Obstinacy, Stupidity, and Illiterature, which leads mortals to dangerous and unexcessible ways; in this last Society, for the most part women are of, as being bred therein, and having such ill Tutors and Guides, they must needs err, for there is an old saying, When the Blind leads the Blind, they must needs fall into the Ditch, not having sight to choose their way; so women breeding up women, the Generations must needs be Fools: for the first, women had an ill Tutor, the Devil, which neither instructed her in the knowledge of Wisdome nor Wit, but learn'd her hurtful dissimulation, to which she hath bred all her Female Generations successively, as from Female to Female; but your question is, whether women are capable of Wit and Wisdome: truly in my opinion women are more capable of Wit than Wisdome, by reason they are both of the Female Gender, which may cause some sympathy in their Natures; and in some things they do plainly sympathy and agree, for Wit is wild and various, and so are women, and Wit is busie and meddles with every thing, cause, or subject, so do women; Wit is fantastical, and so are women, Wit is alwayes in extremes, and so are women, Wit doth talk much, and so do women, Wit is humoursome, and so are women, Wit is prodigal, and so are women, Wit loves praises, and so do women, Wit doth sport and play, dance and sing the time away, and so do women, Wit is many times wanton, and so are women; Thus far are women capable of the Society and Conversation of Wit; but I doubt of her lubtile Invention, quick Apprehension, tare Conceptions, elevated Fancy, and smooth Eloqution.

As for Wisdome, women seem to all outward appearance to have a natural Antipathy abhorring his severe and strict Rules, hating his mediciable Admonitions, his profitable Counsels and Advice, his wary wayes, his prudent forecast, his serious actions, his temperate life and sober disposition; all which makes them uncapable of the Society of Wisdome.

[Exeunt.

Enter **TWO GENTLEMEN**.

FIRST GENTLEMAN
I suppose you have heard that a company of young Gentlemen have set up an Academy, next to the Ladies Academy.

SECOND GENTLEMAN
We heard nothing of it.

FIRST GENTLEMAN
Why then I will tell you, the men are very angry that the women should speak so much, and they so little, I think: for they have made that Room which they stood in to see and hear the Ladies speak in, so a place for themselves to speak in, that the Ladies may hear what they can say.

SECOND GENTLEMAN
Faith if you will have my opinion, it is, that the men do it out of a mockery to the Ladies.

FIRST GENTLEMAN
'Tis likely so, for they rail extremely that so many fair young Ladies are so strictly inclosed, as not to suffer men to visit them in the Academy.

SECOND GENTLEMAN
Faith if the men should be admitted into their Academy, there would be work enough for the Grave Matrons, were it but to act the part of Midwives.

[Exeunt.

Enter the **ACADEMY LADIES**, and their **GRAVE MATRONS**; another of the **YOUNG LADIES** sits as Lady Speaker in an Armed Chair, the rest on stools about her.

MATRON
Lady, at this time let the Theam of your discourse be of discourting.

LADY
As for, Discourse it is differently various, some discourses are delightful and pleasing, others tedious and troublesome, some rude and uncivil, some vain and unnecessary, some gracefull and acceptable, some wise and profitable; but in most discourses time is lost, having nothing that is worthy to be learn'd,

practised, or observed: But there are two sorts of discourses, or manner of wayes of discoursings, as there is a discoursing within the mind, and a discourse with words; as for the inward discourse in the mind, it is to discourse to a mans self, as if they were discoursing to others, making Questions or Propositions, Syllogisms and Conclusions to himself, wherein a man may deceive himself with his own false arguments, for it is an old saying, That it is one thing to oppose himself, and another thing to be opposed by others, and it is easie to argue without opposition; As for discoursing with words, it is more difficult than to discourse with thoughts: for though words are as high and substantial as thoughts, yet the Mouth is not so ready in speaking, as the Brain in thinking, and the Brain can present more thoughts at one time, than the Mouth can deliver words at one time: but words, or Rhetorick is apt to deceive a man, as his Conceptions, especially Orators, which draw themselves with the force of Rhetorick, from the right and the truth, so as an Orator is as apt to delude himself, as to delude his Auditory, if he make words or eloquence the ground of his Questions, Perswasions, or Judgement, and not Reason, for Reason must find out the truth, and right, and Truth must judge the cause; but Rhetorick is for the most part a Vizard to right Reason, for it seems a natural Face, and is not so: Rhetorick seems right Reason, but is not: Also there at extemporal discourses, and discourses premeditated, extemporal sounds best to the ears of the hearers, although of lesse wit than premeditated discourses, because they are delivered more naturally, and so flow more freely and easily, which makes the noise not only to sound more sweetly, but the discourse to be more delightful both to the ears and the mind of the hearers, and more ready to the understanding; but of all discourses the disputive discourses are harshest: Indeed all disputive discourses are like Chromatick Musick, wherein is more Skill than Harmony; but all discourses should be fitted, measured, or chosen to the time, place, persons, and occasions, for that discourse which is proper for one time, place, or person, is improper for another time, place, or person, as a discourse of mirth in a time of sadnesse, a familiar discourse from an Inferior to a Superior, a vain discourse to a serious humour, or an Effeminate discourse to a man, or a Masculine discourse to a woman, and many the like examples might be given: Also there are discourses that are sensible discourses, rational discourses, and witty discourses: also there are other discourses, that have neither Sense, Reason, Wit, nor Fancy in them: Also there are Clownish discourses and Courtly discourses: Also there is a general discoursing, and particular discoursing, also Scholastical discourses and Poetical discourses: but of all the several wayes, manners, or sorts of discourses and discoursings, Let me commend the Poetical discourses and discoursings, which are brief and quick, full of variety, curiosity, and newnesse, being as new as peep of day, as refreshing as the Zephyrus wind, as modest as the blushing morning, sweet as the flowry Spring, as pleasant as a Summers Evening, as profitable as Autumns Harvest, as splenderous as the mid-day Sun, as flowing as the full Tide Sea, as dilating as the spreading Ayre, as fruitfull as the fertile earth, and have as great an influence upon the Natures, Dispositions, and Humours of men, as the Stars, & Planets in the Heavens have, it takes life from the Coelestial flame, and is produced from the Gods on high: and this discourse makes Man resemble to a Deity.

[Exeunt.

SCENE V

Enter **TWO GENTLEMEN** as meeting each other.

FIRST GENTLEMAN
Whither so hastily?

SECOND GENTLEMAN
I am going to hear them speak in the Academy.

FIRST GENTLEMAN
They have done for this time.

SECOND GENTLEMAN
And did they spaek well.

FIRST GENTLEMAN
As they use to do.

SECOND GENTLEMAN
Why they never spake before there!

FIRST GENTLEMAN
Where?

SECOND GENTLEMAN
Why in the Academy.

FIRST GENTLEMAN
Why I am sure I heard one Lady speak yesterday, and another to day.

SECOND GENTLEMAN
Ladies, I mean the Academy of men.

FIRST GENTLEMAN
Why do the men intend to speak?

SECOND GENTLEMAN
Yes presently, if they have not done speaking already.

[Exeunt.

SCENE VI

Enter a Company of **YOUNG MEN**, as in the Room next to the **LADIES**; one takes the Chair.

GENTLEMAN SPEAKER
Gentlemen, we need no Learned Scholars, nor Grave Sages to propound the Theam of our discourse in this place, and at this time; for our minds are so full of thoughts of the Female Sex, as we have no room for any other Subject or Object; wherefore let the Theam be what it will, our discourses will soon run on them: but if we could bring women as easily into our arms, as into our brains; and had we as many Mistresses in our possessions, as we have in our imaginations, we should be much more happy than we

are; Nay, had we been blind, deaf, and insensible to the Sex, we had been happy, unlesse that Sex had been more kinder than they are; but they are cruel, which makes men miserable; but Nature had made Beauty in vain, if not for the use of the Masculine Sex, wherfore Nature forbids restraint, and 'tis a sin against Nature for women to be Incloystred, Retired, or restrained: Nay, it is not only a sin against Nature, but a grievous sin against the Gods, for women to live single lives, or to vow Virginity: for if women live Virgins, there will be no Saints for Heaven, nor worship nor Adoration offred to the Gods from Earth for if all women live Virings, the Race of Mankind will be utterly extinguished; and if it be a general sin to live Virgins, no particular can be exempted; and if it be lawfull for one to live a Virgin, it is lawfull for all; so if it be unlawfull for one, it is unlawfull for all; but surely the Gods would not make any thing lawful that were against themselves: But to conclude, those women which restrain themselves from the company and use of men, are damned, being accused by Men, judged by Nature, and condemned by the Gods.

[Exeunt.

SCENE VII

Enter **TWO GENTLEWOMEN**.

FIRST GENTLEWOMAN
What say you, will you go into the Academy?

SECOND GENTLEWOMAN
No faith, I mean not to be damned.

FIRST GENTLEMAN
I am of your mind, I will run unto the men to save me.

SECOND GENTLEWOMAN
So will I, since the wayes of Salvation are so easie and so pleasant.

[Exeunt.

SCENE VIII

Enter the **ACADEMY OF LADIES**, and the Grave **MATRONNESSE**: The **LADY** that is to speak takes a Chair.

MATRON
Lady, let the Theam of your discourse be at this time on the behaviour of our Sex.

LADY SPEAKER
It is a greater difficulty for a woman to behave her self discreetly in private Visitations, than for a man to speak wisely in privy Councels: and it is a greater difficulty for a woman to behave her self wel in a publick Assembly, than for a man to speak eloquently in a publick Auditory: and it is a greater difficulty

for a woman to behave her self well to several Persons, and in several Assemblies, than for a man to behave himself gallantly in several Battels, and as much dishonour comes in the misbehaviour of the one, as the cowardlinesse of the other: Wherefore there requires as much skill, care, and conduct in a womans behaviour, in visiting, entertaining, placing, applying, and discoursing, as to a Commander in Mustering, Training, Intrenching, Besieging, Inbattelling, Fighting, and Retreating; for it is not enough for a woman to behave her self according to her Degree, Quality, Dignity, Birth, and Breeding, Age, Beauty; Wit, and Fortune; But according to Time, Place, and Occasion, Businesse, and Affairs, as also to the Humours, Capacities, Professions, Dignities, Qualities, Births, Breedings, Fortunes, Ages, and Sexes of those persons she is in Company and Conversation withall: Also in mixt Companies she must have a mixt behaviour, and mixt discourses, as sometimes to one, then to another, according as she can handsomely and civilly apply or addresse her self; and to those that apply and addresse themselves to her: for a woman must not behave her self, or discourse unto a great Lord or Prince, as to a Peasant, or to a Peasant as to a great Lord or Prince, nor to a Souldier as to a Divine, nor to a Divine as to a Souldier, nor to a States-man as to a Tradesman, nor to a Tradesman as to a States-man, nor to a Flattering Gallant, as to a Grave Senior, nor to a Grave Senior as to a Flattering Gallant, nor to a young man as to an antient man, nor to a Boy as to a man, nor to a woman as to a man, nor to a Poet as to a woman, or as to those men that understand not Poetry, nor to learned men, as to ignorant men. Also an antient Grave Matron must not behave her self like a wanton young Girl, nor a Wife like a Maid, nor a Widow like a Wife, nor a Mother like her Daughter, not a Mistriss like her Servant, nor a Servant like a Mistriss, not a great Lady like a Country wise, nor a Country wife like a great Lady, for that would be ridiculous; Indeed it is easier for a middle Rank or Degree, at least it is oftner seen, to behave themselves better than those of high Titles and great Estates, or those of a very mean Condition, and of low Birth, for the one is apt to err with excessive pride, the other with an excessive rudenesse, both being bold and ignorantly bred, knowing not how to be civil, nor what belongs to civil Persons; for the pride of the one scorns to be instructed, and the poverty of the other hath not means to keep and pay Instructers; for the excesse of Plenty nussles the one in Ignorance, and excesse of Poverty blindfolds the other from knowledge: but to conclude of the behaviour of women, first as to the generality, they must behave themselves civilly and circumspectly, to particulars, modestly and friendly; for the chief Principals of behaviour are twelve, six good, and six bad; the six good are, Ceremony, Civility, Modesty, Humility, Friendship, and Obedience: The first is Majestical and Magnificent, the second Noble, the third Virtuous, the fourth Humane, the fift Generous, the sixt Pious; The first is Gracefull, the second Sociable, the third Delightfull, the fourth Natural, the fift Helpfull, the sixt Necessary; The first belongs to Dignity, the second to Breeding, the third to Youth, the fourth to Age, the fift to Wealth, the sixt to Peace.

As for the six bad Principals, is, to be Proud, Bold, Rude, Wanton, Disobedient, and Cruel; The first is, Insolent, the second Impudent, the third Ignorant, the fourth Brutish, the fift Unnatural, the sixt Wicked: The first lives with mean Births, joined with good Fortune, the second lives with ignorant & doltish Spirits, the third with base Breeding, the fourth with Beasts, the fift with uncivil Nations, the sixt with Atheists: The first is to be Slighted, the second to be Pityed, the third to be Shunned, the fourth to be Hated, the fift to be Governed, the sixt to be Punished.

[Exeunt.

SCENE IX

Enter **TWO GENTLEMEN**.

FIRST GENTLEMAN
What say you to these young Ladies?

SECOND GENTLEMEN
I say, that though they be but young Ladies, they discourse like old Women.

[Exeunt.

Enter a Company of **YOUNG GENTLEMEN**: The **GENTLEMEN SPEAKER** takes the Chair.

GENTLEMAN SPEAKER
THE beauty of the Female Sex hath as great an influence upon the eyes of men, as the stars of the Heavens have upon their nature and disposition: but as a cloud of ill Education, covers, changes, or buries the good influence of the Stars; so a cloud of Time covers, changes, and buries the beauties of the fairest Ladies faces, which alters the affections of men, and buries all the delight that was received there-from, in the ruines of age, and the graves of wrinckles: But beauty, whilst it is fresh and flourishing, it is the most powerfull Conqueresse and Triumphs in the Chariot of Youth; and though her Masculine Subjects forsake her, when time hath displaced her, and weakened her power; yet she were unwise, not to take pleasure in her Victories, whilst she may.

[Exeunt.

Enter **TWO CITIZEN WIVES**.

FIRST WIFE
Come, come, Neighbour, we shall get no room to see and hear the young Ladies, if we go not quickly.

SECOND WIFE
Yes, let us go; but stay Neighbour, I must run home again, for I have left the key in the Celar door.

FIRST WIFE
Let it be there for this time.

SECOND WIFE
By my truth I must not, for my maid Joan, and the Prentice, will drink out all my Ale, and strong Beer, and there will be none left to give my Husband a draught when he goeth to bed.

[Enter another **CITIZENS WIFE**.

FIRST WIFE
What, Neighbour, are you come back already?

THIRD WIFE
Why there is no getting in; the Door-keeper beat me back, and said there was no room for Citizens Wives, for the room was only kept for Ladies, and Gentlewomen of Quality.

SECOND WIFE
Well, we may come to be Ladies one day, although not Gentlewomen, and then we shall not so often be beaten back.

FIRST WIFE
Let us go to the Gentlemens side, they will receive us, and use us kindly.

[Exeunt.

SCENE XII

Enter the **ACADEMY OF YOUNG LADIES**, and their **MATRONS**. They all sit, and the **LADY SPEAKER** takes the Chair.

MATRON
Ladies, let the Theam of our discourse, at this time, be of Truth.

LADY SPEAKER
Truth, although she hath but one face, which is a natural face, yet she hath many several countenances; for somtimes her countenance is severe, other times kind and familiar, sometimes it is sad, sometimes merry, other times pleasing and delightfull: also she hath as different humours, as she hath countenances, according to the Cause, or Occasion; likewise, her presence, or approach, shews the different Effects, and several Causes; or from one Cause on several Objects, or Subjects: As for Example, sometimes her Approach shews man to be Miserable, or Happy; as when she comes to inform him of good Fortune, or bad; or when she presents him with right Understanding of the condition he is in: But in Truth, in whatsoever countenance, or humour she puts on, she is a most beautifull Lady: for although she do not shine as the Sun, which dazles and obscures the sight with his splendrous beams, yet she doth appear like a bright, clear day, wherein, and whereby, all things are seen perfectly; and although she have various Humours, yet her Actions are just, for the alteration of her Countenance, and Humours, are not to deceive men, nor she takes no delight in her own sad Approach, to grieve men, but she doth bear a-part, both of their Grief and Joy: she makes neither the Chances, Fortunes, Accidents nor Actions, but only declares them: she is neither the Cause, nor Effects, but only shews the several Effects of Causes, or what causes those Effects: She is of a sweet Nature, and an humble Disposition, she doth as freely, and commonly accompany the Poor, as the Rich, the Mean as the Great: Indeed, her constant Habitation and dwelling, is among the Learned and Industrious men; but she hath an opposite or rival, namely Falshood, which often obscures her, and is often preferr'd before her: this Falshood, her Rival, is of the nature of a Curtezan, as all Curtezans are, as to flatter, and insinuate her self and company, to all mens good liking, and good opinion: she is full of deceit and dissembling, and although she hates Truth, yet she imitates her as much as she can; I do not say she imitates the Justice, Severity,

and Plainesse of Truth; for those, of all things, or actions, she shuns; but she imitates her Behaviour and Countenance; for although Falshood is fowl, and filthy of her self, yet by artificial Paint, she makes herself appear as fair, and pure as Truth; but the deservingly Wise can soon see the difference between the artificial fair of Falshood, and the true, natural, fair complexion of Truth, although fools do admire, and are sooner catch'd, so, for the most part deceived with the deceiving Arts of Falshood, than the natural Verity of Truth: for Falshood makes a glaring shew at the first sight, but the more she is viewed, the worse she appears; whereas Truth, the more she is viewed, the better she appears: also Falshood uses Rhetorick, to allure and deceive with her Eloquent Tongue, whereas Truth speaks little her self, but brings alwaies, and at all times, and in all places, and to all things, Right Reason, and plain Proof to speak for her, who speak without flourishing Phrases, or decking Sentences, or Scholastical Rules, Methods or Tenses, but speak to the purpose, deliver the matter briefly, and keep to the sense of Truth, or true sense, which is both the best and natural way of speaking, and the honest Practice of Truth, whereas Eloquence is one of the most cozening and abusing Arts as is; for as Paint is a Vizard on the face, so is Eloquence a Vizard on the mind, and the Tongue is the Pencil of Deceit, drawing the Pictures of Discourse; thus Falshood strives to resemble Truth, as much as artificially she can.

[Exeunt.

ACT III

SCENE XIII

Enter **TWO GENTLEMEN**.

FIRST GENTLEMAN
How do you like the Ladies and their discoursings?

SECOND GENTLEMAN
I like some of the Ladies discourses better than others; and I like some of the Ladies better than the other; but let us go hear the men.

[Exeunt.

SCENE XIV

Enter a Company of **GENTLEMEN**, he that is to speak takes the Chair.

GENTLEMAN SPEAKER
Those women that retire themselves from the Company of men, are very ungratefull; as, first to Nature, because she made them only for breed; next to men who are their Defenders, Protectors, their Nourishers, their Maintainers, their Instructers, their Delighters, their Admirers, their Lovers and Deifiers; as men defend them from the raging blustring Elements, by building them Houses, and not only build them Houses for shelter, but Houses for pleasure and magnificency: Also men protect them from wild ravenous and cruel Beasts, that otherwise would devour them; for as women have not natural

strength to build, so have they not natural courage to fight, being for the most part as fearfull as weak: Likewise men nourish them, for men Fish Fowl, and hunt to get them Food to feed them, for which women would neither take the pains, nor indure the labour, nor have the heart to kill their food; for women by nature are so pittifull, and have such tender dispositions, as they would rather suffer death themselves, than destroy life in other Creatures; Also men maintain them by composing themselves into Commonwealths, wherein is Traffique and Commerce, that each Family may live by each other; Also Laws to keep them in peace, to rule them in order, to defend them with Arms, which women could never do, by reason they know not what Government to settle in or to, nor what Laws to make, or how to execute those Laws that were made; neither could they plead Sutes, decide Causes, Judge Controversies, deal out right, or punish Injuries, or condemn Criminals: Also men are the Instructers to inform them of Arts and Sciences, which women would nere have had the patience to study, for they would never have allowed so much time and solitary musing, for the perfecting or delivering those Conceptions, as those that first invented or found them out; besides if women were not instructed by men of the natural cause of Effects, how often would they have been affrighted almost to death, with the loud and terrifying Thunders, the flashing Lightenings, the dark Eclipses, the unsteady Earthquakes, the overflowing Tides, and many the like natural Effects from hidden Causes? besides, women would want all those conveniencies that Art affords them, and furnishes them with: Also men instruct women with the Mystery of the Gods, whereas for want of which knowledge, they would have been damned through ignorance: Also men are their Delighters, they traffique on the Sea, all over the world, to every several Climate and Country, to find and to bring the Female Sex Curiosities, hazarding their lives for the same; whereas women could neither build their Ships, nor guide them on the Seas when they were built; they have not strength to pull and tug great Cable Ropes, to set and spread large Sails, to cast and weigh Massy Anchors, no, not in a calm, much lesse in furious storms, with which men often fight, though not with Arms, with Subtility and Skill, by which the Elements are conquered still, whereas women are conquered, and not only being strengthlesse and heartlesse, but healthlesse; for not only the roaring Seas, and whistling winds, and ratling showres, and rumbling Thunders, and fiery Lightenings, Rocks, Shelves, and Sands unknown, or not to be avoided, besides Mountains of Ice, if to the Northern Pole, all which would terrifie them, yet their weak bodies, sick stomacks, and nice Appetites, could never endure long Voyages; they would vomit out their life before they could sayl to their assigned Port, or Haven: Also men are womens admirers, they gaze on their Beauties, and praise their sweet Graces, whereas women through envy detract from each other; Also men are womens only True Lovers, they flatter, kisse and please them, whereas women are apt to quarrel, rail and fight with each other: And lastly, men Deifie women, making them Goddesses by their Poetical Descriptions & Elevations, whereas Nature made them meer Mortals, Human creatures; wherefore it is a great ingratitude, nay a horid ingratitude in those women, that denye men their Company, Conversation, and Communication; wherefore men have not only Reason to take it ill, but to be angry with those women that shun or restrain their Company from them; but good Counsel ought to go before Anger, for the difference betwixt good Counsel and Anger, is, that good Counsel goes before a fault is committed, and Anger followeth when a fault is committed, for as good Counsel or Admonishment is to prevent a fault, so Anger is a Punishment for a fault past.

[Exeunt.

SCENE XV

Enter **THREE ANTIENT LADIES.**

FIRST LADY
Is your Daughter put into the Academy?

SECOND LADY
Yes.

THIRD LADY
How long Madam hath your Daughter been in the Academy?

SECOND LADY
This week, but she hath not profited much, for I do not hear her discourse.

FIRST LADY
First it is to be considered, whether your Daughter be capable of discoursing, for she must have a natural ingenuity to the Art of Rhetorick.

THIRD LADY
My Daughter was always a pretty talking Girl, as any in all the Country and Town I lived in.

SECOND LADY
Yes, Children may talk prettily for Children, but when they come to be women, it is a question whether they will talk wisely or no; but let us go hear which of the Ladies discourses to day.

[Exeunt.

SCENE XVI

Enter the **ACADEMICAL LADIES** and their **MATRONS**; The **LADY SPEAKER** takes the Chair.

MATRON
Lady, for this time let the Theam of your discourse be of Discourse.

LADY SPEAKER
Reverend Matron, this Theam hath been discoursed of before by one of our Academy; but yet by reason one and the same Theam may be discoursed of after different manners or wayes, I shall obey you.
As for Discourse, there is of four sorts; the first is discoursing in the mind, which is reasoning.
The second is discoursing with words, which is speaking,
The third is discoursing by signs, which is action or acting.
The last is discoursing by Figures, which is by Letters and Hieroglyphicks, which is by Printing, Writing, Painting, and the like.

As for the first, which is a discourse in the mind, which is Reasoning, which reasoning is a discourse with things, and not with words, as such a thing is not such a thing, and what such things are, and what they are not, or in what such things agreee or disagree, sympathy, or antipathy, or such things resemble, or not resemble, or on the cause of things, or their effects, or the like: This discourse is in the mind, which is distinguishing, and distinguishing belongs to Judgement.

The second discoursing is with words, which is Speech, and words are not things, but only marks of things, or nicks, or notches to know things by; and the Tongue is the Tally on which they are scored: for Speech is a number of words, which words are made and joyned together by the Breath, Tongue, Teeth, and Lips, and the continuance make a discourse; for a discourse is like a line or thread, whereon are a number of words strung, like as a Chain of Beads, if the words be well sorted, and fitly and properly matched, as also evenlystrung, the discourse is pleasant and delightfull; this Chain of discourse is longer or shorter, according as the Speaker pleases. The third discourse, is a discourse by Signes, which is in Actions, as some can discourse by the Motion of their Faces, Countenances, Hands, Fingers, Paces, or Measures, or by the cast of the Eyes, and many such like Postures, Looks, Actions, and several such wayes of Motion as have been invented to be understood. This and the first kind of discourse, as by things and motions, beasts may have, for ought we can know to the contrary. The last is by Figures, or Letters, Prints, Hieroglyphicks, and painted Stories, or ingraven in Metal, or cur, or carved in Stone, or molded, or formed in Earth, as clay, or the like; in this kind of discourse, the Pencil hath sometimes out-done the Pen, as the Painter hath out-done the Historian and Poet: This discoursing by Signs, or Figures, are discourses to the eye, and not to the ear. There is also another kind, or sort of discoursing, which is hardly learn'd as yet, because newly invented, or at lest, to what I have heard, which is by Notes, and several Strains in the Musick. I only mention it, because I never heard it but once, and then I did not understand it: but yet it was by a skilfull and ingenious Musician, which discoursed a story of his Travels, in his playing on a Musical Instrument, namely, the Harpsical. But certainly, to my understanding, or reason, it did seem a much easier way of discoursing, than discoursing by actions, or posture. But to end my discourse of Discoursing, which discoursing may by several waies, several actions and postures, by several creatures, and in several Languages: but reasoning is the Souls Language, words the Language of the Senses, action the Lifes Language, Writing, Printing, Painting, Carving and Molding, are Arts several Languages, but Musick is the Language of the Gods.

[Exeunt.

SCENE XVII

Enter **TWO GENTLEMEN**.

FIRST GENTLEMAN
How do you like the Ladies discourse?

SECOND GENTLEMAN
As I like discourse.

FIRST GENTLEMAN
How is that?

SECOND GENTLEMAN
Why I had rather hear a number of words, than speak a number of words.

FIRST GENTLEMAN
Then thou art not of the nature of Mankind; for there is no man that had not rather speak than hear.

SECOND GENTLEMAN
No, it is a sign I am not of the nature of Woman-kind, that will hear nothing, but will speak all; indeed, for the most part, they stop their Ears with their Tongues, at lest, with the sound of their Voices.

[Exeunt.

SCENE XVIII

Enter a company of **GENTLEMEN**; The **SPEAKER** takes the Chair.

GENTLEMAN SPEAKER
IT were too tedious to recite the several humours of the female Sex; their scornfull Pride, their obstinate Retirednesse, their reserved Coynesse, their facil Inconstancy, by which they become the most useless, and most unprofitable Creatures that nature hath made; but when they are joined to men, they are the most usefull, and most profitable Creatures nature hath made; wherefore, all those women that have common reason, or sense of shame, will never retire themselves from the company of men: for what women that have any consideration of Hononr, Truth, or touch of Goodness, will be the worst of all Creatures, when they may be the best? but the truth of it is, women are spoyled by the over-fond dotage of men; for being flattered, they become so self-conceited, as they think they were only made for the Gods, and not for men; and being Mistrisses of mens affections, they usurp their Masculine Power and Authority, and instead of being dutifull, humble and obedient to men, as they ought to be, they are Tyrannical Tyrannizers.

[Exeunt.

SCENE XIX

Enter **TWO GENTLEMEN**.

FIRST GENTLEMAN
THE young Gallants methinks begin to be whetted with Anger.

SECOND GENTLEMAN
They have reason, when the women have such dull, blunt Appetites.

[Exeunt.

SCENE XX

Enter the **LADIES OF THE ACADEMY**: The **LADY SPEAKER** takes the Chair.

MATRON
Ladies, let the Theam of your discourse be, at this time, of Friendship.

LADY SPEAKER
This Theam may more easily be discoursed of, than Friendship made; by reason it is very difficult to make a right Friendship, for hard it is to match men in agreeable Humours, Appetites, Passions, Capacities, Conversations, Customs, Actions, Natures and Dispositions, all which must be to make a true and lasting Friendship, otherwise, two Friends will be like two Horses that draw contrary waies, whereas Souls, Bodies, Education and Lives, must equally agree in Friendship; for a worthy honest man cannot be a friend to a base and unworthy man, by reason Friendship is both an offensive and defensive League between two Souls and Bodies; and no actions, either of the Souls or Bodies, or any outward thing, or fortune belonging thereunto, are to be denyed; wherefore Knaves with Knaves, and unworthy Persons with unworthy Persons, may make a Friendship, & Honest men with Honest men, and worthy Persons with worthy Persons, may do the like: but an Honest man with a Knave, or a worthy Person with a base man, or an Honourable Person with a mean Fellow, a noble Soul with a base Nature, a Coward with a Valiant man, can make no true Friendship. For, put the case, in such friendships, my Friend should desire me to do a base Action for his sake, I must either speak break Friendship, or do unworthily, but as all worthy Persons make Truth their Godesse, which they seek and worship, Honour the Saint which they pray too, Vertue, the Lady which they serve, so Honesty is the only Friend they trust and rely on, and all the World is obliged to Honesty, for upright and just dealing.

[Exeunt.

ACT IV

SCENE XXI

Enter **TWO GENTLEMEN**.

FIRST GENTLEMAN
Methinks the womens Lectural discourse is better than the mens; for in my opinion, the mens discourses are simple, childish, and foolish, in comparison of the womens,

SECOND GENTLEMAN
Why, the subject of the discourse is of women, which are simple, foolish, and childish.

FIRST GENTLEMAN
There is no sign of their simplicity or folly, in their discourse or Speeches, I know not what may be in their Actions.

SECOND GENTLEMAN
Now you come to the point, for the weaknesse of women lyes in their Actions, not in their Words, for they have sharp Wits and blunt Judgements.

[Exeunt.

Enter the **LADIES** and Grave **MATRONESS**; The **LADY SPEAKER** takes the Chair.

MATRONESSE
Lady, let the Theam of your discourse to day be of a Theatre.

LADY SPEAKER
A Theatre is a publick place for publick Actions, Orations, Disputations, Presentations, whereunto is a publick resort; but there are only two Theatres, which are the chief, and the most frequented; the one is of War, the other of Peace; the Theatre of Warr is the Field; and the Battels they sight, are the Plays they Act, and the Souldiers are the Tragedanis, and the Theatre of Peace is the stage, and the Plays there Acted are the Humours, Manners, Dispositions, Natures, Customes of men thereon described and acted, whereby the Theatres are as Schools to teach Youth good Principles, and instruct them in the Nature and Customes of the World and Mankind, and learn men to know themselves better than by any other way of instruction; and upon these Theatres, they may learn what is noble and good, what base and wicked, what is ridiculous and misbecoming, what gracefull and best becoming, what to avoid and what to imitate; the Genius that belongs to the Theatre of Warr is Valour, and the Genius that belongs to the Theatre of Peace is Wit; the designer of the rough Plays of Warr, is a General or Councel; the designer of the smooth Plays of Peace is a Poet, or a chief Magistrate; but the difference of these Plays Acted on each Theatre, is, the one is real, the other feigned, the one in earnest, the other in jest; for a Poet only feigns Tragedies, but the Souldiers do truly act Tragedies; on the Poetical Theatre I will only insist, for this Theatre belongs more to our persons, and is a more fitter Subject for the discourse of our Sex, than Warr is; for we delight more in Scenes than in Battels: I will begin first with Poets, who are the Authors and makers of these kind of Plays; Fame hath spoke loud, both of antient and modern Poets; as for the antient Poets, they are a length out of the reach of my Judgement, so as my opinion will hardly reach so far; but as for our Modern Poets, that have made Plays in our Modern times, although they deserve praise, yet not so much nor so high Applause as is given them; for most of their Plots, or Foundation of their Plays, were taken out of old Authors, as from the Greeks and Romans, Historians and Poets, also all the Modern Romances are taken out of these Stories, and many Playes out of these Romances.

MATRON
Lady, give me leave a little while to instruct you, as to tell you, that all Romances should be so; for the ground of a right Romance is a true story, only falshood is intermixt therein, so that a Romance is a compound of Truth and Falshood.

LADY SPEAKER
Give me leave to answer you, that in my opinion, a right Romance is Poetical Fictions put into a Historical Stile; but for Plays, the true Comedy is pure Love and Humours, also the Customes, Manners, and the Habits, and inbred qualities of mankind; And right Tragi-Comedies are the descriptions of the Passions which are created in the Soul; And a right Tragedy is intermixt with the Passions, Appetites, and Humours of men, with the influence of outward actions, accidents, and misfortunes: but as I said, some Poets take the Plots out of true History, others out of feigned Historie, which are Romances, so as their Plots (for the most part) are meer Translations, and oft times the Wit is also but a translated Wit, only

metamorphosed after their own way; but the truth is, that some of them their Wit is their own, and their Plots were stoln, or plainly taken, and some their Plots are their own, but the Wit stoln; but of all theft, Wit is never confest; and some neither the Plot nor Wit is their own, and others both Plots and Wit are truly their own; These last Poets (although but very few) are the true Sons of Nature, the other but as adulterate issues; But for the most part, our Modern Plays, both Plots and Wit, are meer translations, and yet come out as boldly upon the Stage, as if the Translators were the Original Authors, thinking, or at least hoping that the alteration of the Language conceals the theft, which to the unlearued it doth, but the learned soon find them out, and see all their Bodies, Wings, Leggs, Tail, and Feathers, although they hide their head in the Bush of Ignorance. I speak not in discommendation of these Translations, nor Translators, for Translations are so far from being condemned, as they ought to be much, nay very much commended, and highly praised, if it be such as is praise worthy, for old Authors may in some expressions be more profitable and good, both for Wit and Examples, than the modern; and the Translators may be commended both for their Judgement and Learning; besides, very good Translators must have a sympathetical Genius, with the Original Author, but their Condemnation proceeds from the Translators unjust owning of it, upon themselves, or in translating it to the Authors prejudice.

MATRON
Lady, let me interrupt you once again, to ask your opinion how you like the Italian and French Plays.

LADY SPEAKER
As well as I can like any thing that is a strain beyond Nature, or as I may say, Natures Constraint: for the truth is, in their discourse or rehearsals, they do not only raise their Voice a Note or two too high, but many Notes too high, and in their actions they are so forced, as the Spectators might very easily believe the Actors would break their Sinewstrings; and in their Speech they fetch their breath so short and thick, and in such painfull fetches and throws, as those Spectators that are Strangers, might verily believe that they were gasping for life.

MATRON
But Lady, all know Love, which is the Theam or Subject of Plays, is a violent passion, which forces the Players to an Elevation of Action and Speech.

LADY SPEAKER
Most Reverend Matron, my opinion is, that though it be commendable and admirable for the Poet to be elevated with a Poetical Divine Inspiration to outdo Nature; yet for the Actors, their best grace is to Play or Act in the Tracts or Paths of Nature, and to keep within Natures bounds; and whensoever they go awry, or transgresse therefrom, they are to be condemned, and to be accounted ill Actors; and as for the Passions of Love, certainly the strongest Love is like the deepest Water, which is most silent, and least unnecessarily active; they may sometimes murmur, with winds of sighs, but never roar; they neither foam nor froth with violence, but are composed into a heavy body, with a setled sadnesse: But in short, the Italian and French Players act more Romantical than Natural, which is feign'd and constrain'd: but to conclude with the Poet, he delights the Ear and the Understanding with the variety of every thing that Nature, hath made, or Art invented; for a Poet is like a Bee, that gathers the sweet of every Flower, and brings the Hony to his Hive, which are the Ears and Memory of the Hearers, or Readers, in whose Head his Wit swarms; but as Painters Draw to the life, so Poets should Write to the life, and Players Act to the life.

[Exeunt.

SCENE XXIII

Enter **THREE GENTLEMEN**.

FIRST GENTLEMAN
The Academy of Ladies take no notice of the Academy of Men, nor seem to consider what the men say, for they go on their own serious way, and edifying discourses.

SECOND GENTLEMAN
At which the men are so angry, as they have sworn to leave off talking, and instead thereof, they will sound Trumpets so loud, when the Ladys are in their discoursings, as they shall not hear themselves speak; by which means they hope to draw them out of their Cloyster, as they swarm Bees; for as Bees gather together at the sound of a Basin, Kettle, or such like metled thing: so they will disperse that swarm of Academical Ladies, with the sound of brazen Trumpets.

THIRD GENTLEMAN
Why the Ladies look through their Grate, upon the men, whilst the men are speaking, and seem to listen to what they speak, as the men do on and to the Ladies.

SECOND GENTLEMAN
That is true, but they take no notice of them in their literal Discourses, as what the men have said; for they neither mention the men, nor their Discoursing, or Arguments, or Academy, as if there were no such men.

[Exeunt.

SCENE XXIV

Enter the **LADIES**, and their **MATRONS**: The **LADY SPEAKER** takes the Chair.

MATRON
Lady, let the Theam of your discourse be, at this time, of Vanity, Vice, and Wickedness.

LADY SPEAKER
There is a difference betwixt Vanity, Vice, and Wickednesse: Wickednesse is in the will, Vice in the desires, and Vanity in the actions Will proceeds from the Soul, Vice from the Appetites, and Action from Custom, or Practice; the Soul is produced from the Gods, the Appetites created by Nature, and Custom is derived from Time: As for Desires, we may desire, and not will, and we may will, and not act, and we may act, and neither will, nor desire, and we may desire, will, and act all at once; and to some particulars, we may neither desire, will nor act; but the Will makes Vice Wickednesse, and Vanity Vice; the willing of good, proceeds from the Gods, the willing of evil proceeds from the Devils: so that Sin is to will evil, in despight of good, and Piety is to will good, in despight of evil, as neither the perswasions, nor temptations of the one, or the other, shall draw our wills; for sin, or wickednesse, is neither in the

Knowledg, nor Appetites: for if our Great Grandmother Eve, had not wilfully eat of that which was strictly forbidden her, she had not sinned, for if that she had only heard of the effects of that Fruit, or had desired it, yet had not wilfully eaten thereof, she had never damned her Posterity: Thus, to will against the Gods command, is Wickednesse: but there is no such thing as Wickedness, in Nature, but as I said Wickednesse proceeds from the Soul, Vice from the Appetites, and Vanity from the Actions: as for Wickedness, it is like a dead Palsie, it hath no sense, or feeling of the Grace or Goodness of the Gods, and Vice is like an unwholsome Meat, cut out by the Appetites, for the Appetites are like knives, whereas some are blunt, others are sharp, and as it were, too much edged, but they are either blunt, or sharp, according as Nature whets them: but if they be very sharp, as to be keen, they wound the body, and make the life bleed. As for Vanity, it is as the froath of life, it is light, and swims a-top, which bubbles out into extravagant and unprofitable actions, false opinions, and idle, and impossible Imaginations. But as I said, it is not the knowledg of Vanity, Vice and Wickednesse, that makes a creature guilty thereof, but the Will, and wilfull Practice thereof, for Wickedness, Vice, and Vanity, must be known as much as Piety, Virtue, and Discretion, otherwise men may run into evil, through ignorance, wherefore it is as great a shame to Education, not to be instructed in the bad, as it is a glory to be instructed in the good: but the Question will be, whether Knowledg can be without a partaking thereof? I Answer, not a perfect Knowledg, but a suppositive Knowledg: for there are many things which cannot be perfectly known, but suppositively known: so we must only know Wickedness, Vice, and Vanity, as we do know the Gods and Devils, which is by a lively Faith; so as we must be instructed in all that is Pious, Virtuous, and Judicious, as we are instructed of the Power and Goodnesse of the Gods; and we must be instructed in all that is Wicked, Vicious, and Idle, as we are of the Evil, and Power of the Devils. Now I must inform you, that there are three sorts of Knowledge, as a knowledge of Possession, a knowledge of Action, and a knowledge of Declaration; the knowledge of Action lies in the Appetites, the knowledge of Declaration lies in the Senses, the knowledge of Possession in the Will, Action and Declarations. As for example, we may hear, and see, Drunkenesse, Adultery, Murther, Theft, and the like, and have no appetite to the same Actions; also we may have an appetite to the same Actions, yet not a will to act the same; but if we have a destre, and will act the same; we have, and are possess'd with the most perfect Knowledge thereof; but this last Knowledge is utterly unlawfull in things that are evil, but not in things that are good: But to conclude, we must be instructed by a Narrative way, and by the intelligence of our ears, and eyes, in that which is evil, as well, and as plainly, as in things that are good, not to be ignorant in any thing that can be declared unto us, not staying untill we be Old, but to be thus instructed whilst we are young; for many that are young Novices, commit many evils through ignorance, not being instructed, and informed plainly and clearly, but darkly, and obscurely, caused by their foolish, cautionary, formal Tutors, or Educators, who hold that erronious opinion, that Youth ought not to know such, or such Things, or Acts; which if they had known, evil might have been prevented, and not left until their evil be known by Practice; so that more evil is rather known by Practice, than Declaration, or instruction of Information: but if our Senses are a guide to our Reason, and our Reason a guide to our Understanding, and that the Reason and Understanding governs our Appetites, then tis probable, our Sense, Reason, and Understanding, may govern our Will.

[Exeunt.

ACT V

SCENE XXV

Enter the **ACADEMICAL GENTLEMEN**.

FIRST GENTLEMAN
ThiS is not to be suffered: for if we should let these Ladies rest in peace and quiet, in their inclosed Habitation, we shall have none but Old Women; for all those young Ladies, that are not in the Academy, talk of nothing but of going into a Female Academy.

SECOND GENTLEMAN
You say true, insomuch as it begins to be a Mode, and a Fashion; for all the Youngest, Fairest, Richest, and Noblest Ladies, to inclose themselves into an Academy.

THIRD GENTLEMAN
Nay, we must seek some way, and devise some means to unroost them.

FOURTH GENTLEMAN
There is nothing can do it, but noise; for they take such pleasure in the exercise of their Tongues, that unless we can put them to silence, there is no hopes to get them out.

FIRST GENTLEMAN
Trumpets, I doubt, will not be loud enough.

SIXTH GENTLEMAN
Let us try.

ALL THE GENTLEMEN
Content, Content, &c.

[Exeunt.

SCENE XXVI

Enter the **LADIES**, and the Grave **MATRONS**; The **LADY SPEAKER** takes the Chair.

MATRON
Lady, let the Theam of your discourse be, at this time, of Boldness, and Bashfulnesse.

LADY SPEAKER
There are three sorts of Boldness, or Confidence, the one proceeds from Custom, or Practice, as it may be observed by Preachers, Pleaders, and Players, that can present themselves, speak, and act freely, in a publick Assembly.

The second sort of Boldnesse, or Confidence, proceeds from Ignorance, not foreseeing what errors, or follies, may be committed, or chance to fall out, or what is fittest to be done, or said; like as poor mean Countrey people, who have neither Birth nor Breeding, have so much Confidence, as they can more confidently present themselves, or presence, to those of Noble Birth and Breeding, and can more freely, and boldly, talk to any Person, or Persons, of what Quality, or Dignity soever, than those Noble Persons can talk to them.

The third, and last sort of Confidence, or Boldnesse, proceeds from an extraordinary Opinionatedness, or self-conceitednesse; for those that think, or believe themselves to be above others, in Wit, Person, Parts, or Power, although they have neither, will be most haughtily, and proudly confident, scorning, and undervaluing all others, as inferiour. Thus bold Confidence, or confident Boldnesse, is produced from Practice, Ignorance, and Pride.

Also there are three sorts of Bashfulnesse.
The one proceeds from too great an Apprehension.
The other from a poetical Fiction.
The third from an aspiring Ambition.

First, from too great an Apprehension, as some are afraid that their Observers, or Friends, should make an evil Construction of their good Intentions. Others will be Bashfull, and out of Countenance, upon a poetical Fiction, as imagining of some impossible, or at least some improbable accident, which may fall out to their disgrace. The third and last is through an aspiring Ambition, desiring to out-act all others in Excellencies, and fearing to fail therein, is apt to be out of Countenance, as if they had received a foyl; thus we may perceive that the Stream of good Nature, the peircing Beams of Wit, and the Throne of Noble Ambition is the true cause of bashfulness, I mean not shamefastness, but sweet bashfulnesse: but although bashfulnesse is a sweet, tender, noble, and peircing Effect, of and from the Soul; yet bashfulnesse is apt to unstring the Nerves, to weaken the Sinews, to dull the Senses, to quench the Spirits, to blunt the eyes or points of Wit, and to obstruct the Speech, insomuch as to cause the words to run stumblingly out of the mouth, or to suffer none to passe forth: but a little Anger in the Mind will take off the extreme bashfulnesse of the Behaviour, although much Anger doth obstruct the Senses, Spirits and Speech, as much as extreme Bashfulnesse doth: for extreme anger, and extreme bashfulnesse, have often one and the same Effects to outward Appearance.

[Exeunt.

SCENE XXVII

Enter **TWO GENTLEMEN**.

FIRST GENTLEMAN
The Gentlemen will turn Trumpeters, for a Regiment of Gentlemen have bought every one of them a Trumpet, to sound a March to the Academy of Ladies.

SECOND GENTLEMAN
Faith if the Ladies would answer their Trumpets with blowing of Horns, they would serve them but as they ought to be served.

FIRST GENTLEMAN
Women will sooner make Hornes, than blow Horns.

[Exeunt

Enter the **LADY** and their **MATRONESS**; The **LADY SPEAKER** takes the Chair.

MATRON
Lady, let the Theam of your discourse at this time be of Virtuous Courtships, and wooing Suters.

LADY SPEAKER
Some Poetical and Romantical Writers make valiant gallant Heroicks wooe poorly, sneakingly, and pedlingly.

MATRON
Lady, let me interrupt you; would you have gallant Heroicks in their Courtships to Fair young Ladies, as Commanding as in the Field, or as Furious as in a Battel.

LADY SPEAKER
No, I would have them wooe with a Confident Behaviour, a Noble Demeanor, a Generous Civility, and not to be amazed or to tremble for fear, to weep for pitty, to kneel for mercy, to sigh and be dejected with a Mistresses frown; for though sorrow, sighs, tears and Humility become all Heroick Spirits very well, and expresse a Noble and Generous Soul, yet not in such a cause: for tears become all Heroick Spirits, for the Death or Torments of Friends, or for the sufferances of Innocents, or Virtue, yet not if only themselves were tormented, or to dye, or for any misfortune that could come upon our own Persons or estates, or for any obstructions to their own pleasures or delights, but it becomes all Heroick Spirits, to tremble for fear of their Honour, or losse of their Fame, and expresses a generous Soul to grieve and to mourn in a general Calamity, and to humble themselves to the Gods for those in distresse, and to implore and kneel to them for mercy, both for themselves and others, as for to divert the wrath of the Gods; but not to weep, sigh, tremble, kneel, pray, for their Effeminate pleasures, delights, or Societies; nor to grieve or sorrow for the losse of the same.

Also some Writers, when they are to describe a Bashfull and Modest Lady, such as are Nobly and Honourably bred, describe them as if they were simply shame faced; which description makes such appear, as if they came meerly from the Milk-boul, and had been bred only with silly Huswives, and that their practice was to pick Worms from Roots of Flowers, and their pastimes to carry and fling crumbs of Bread to Birds, or little Chickens that were hatched by their Hens their Mothers gave them, or to gather a lapfull of sweet Flowers, to Distill a little sweet Water to dip their Hankerchiefs in, or to wash their Faces in a little Rose-water; and indeed, this harmlesse and innocent Breeding, may be Modest and Bashfull, or rather shame-faced, for want of other Conversation, which Custome and Company will soon cast off, or wear out, and then print Boldnesse on their brow; but true modest Souls, which have for the most part Bashfull Countenances, proceed from a deep Apprehension, a clear Understanding, an ingenuous Wit, a thinking Brain, a pure Mind, a refined Spirit, a Noble Education, and not from an ignorant obscure Breeding; for it is not Ignorance that makes Modesty, but Knowledge, nor is it Guiltinesse that makes Bashfulnesse, but fear of those that are guilty; but as I said, many Writers that would make a description of Modest and Bashfull women, mistake and expresse a shame-faced Ignorance and obscure Breeding; and instead of expressing a young Lady to be innocent of Faults, they expresse her to be one that is ignorant of Knowledge, so as when they would describe a Modest, Bashfull, Innocent Virgin, they mistake and describe a simple ignorant shame fac'd Maid, that either wants Breeding or Capacity.

MATRON
But Lady, let me ask you one question, would you have a young Virgin as confident and knowing as a Married Wife?

LADY SPEAKER
Yes, although not in their Behaviour or Condition of life, but in her Virtue and Constancy; for a chast Married wife is as Modest and Bashfull as a Virgin, though not so simple, ignorant, and shame-faced as a plain bred Maid; but as I said, Writers should describe the wooing of gallant Heroicks, or Great and Noble Persons, to woo with a Generous Confidence, or Manly Garb, a Civil Demeanor, a Rational Discourse, to an honest Design, and to a Virtuous end, and not with a whining Voice, in pittifull words, and fawning Language; and if it be only for a Mistriss, as for a Courtezan, Bribes are the best Advocates, or to imploy others to treat with them, and not to be the Pimp, although for themselves.

Also Writers should when they describe Noble Virgins, to receive Noble Addresses of Love, and to receive those Noble Addresses or Courtships with an attentive Modesty in a bashfull Countenance; and if to tremble for fear, to describe the fear, as being the Nature of the Sex; also to describe their Behaviour after a Noble Garb, and their answers to their Suters, to be full of Reason, Sense, and Truth, and those answers to be delivered in as short discourses, and as few words as Civility will allow of, and not like an ignorant innocent, a childish simplicity, an unbred Behaviour, expressing themselves, or answering their Suters with mincing words that have neither Sense nor Reason in them.

Also Poetical and Romantical Writers should not make great Princes that have been bred in great and populous Cities, glorious Camps; and splendrous Courts, to woo and make Love like private bred men, or like rude bred Clowns, or like mean bred Servants, or like Scholars, that woo by the Book in Scholastical Terms or Phrases, or to woo like flanting, ranting, swearing, bragging Swaggerers, or Rusters; or to woo a Country wench, like as a Noble Lady, or great Princesse.

Also not to make such women as have been bred and born Nobly and Honourably, to receive the Courtship of great Persons, like a Dairy-maid, Kitchin-maid, or like such as have been bred in mean Cottages, as to behave themselves simply, or rudely, as to the answer and speak Crossingly, or Thwartingly, as contradicting every word that is spoken unto them, as if they did believe what they said was not truth; for Civil and Honourable bred women, who have Noble and Generous Souls, will rather seem to believe all their Superlative Praises, than make Doubts, as if they knew they lyed; for to make Doubts, is in the mid-way to give the Lye.

MATRON
Lady, how approve you of those Lovers that kisse the Letters, Tokens, Pledges, and the like, that are sent unto them from their Lovers? or such as wear Letters, Tokens, or Pledges in their Bosomes, and next their Hearts, and take them and view them a hundred times a day?

LADY SPEAKER
Approve it say you? you mean disapprove it; but let me tell you, most Reverend Matron, that the very hearing of it makes me sick, and the seeing of it would make me die.

I have so great an Aversion against such actions, for those actions: like as whining Speeches, proceed from filthy Amorous Love, and Mean Lovers; for true Love in Noble Persons, receives gifts as an expression of their Suters, or Lovers Loves, and will carefully keep them as an acknowledgment of the receipt, and accept of them as a great Seal to their affections; yet they keep such Presents, but as Treasurers, not as Owners, untill they be man and wife; neither do they make Idols of such gifts, nor do they adore the Owner the more for the gift, nor the gift for the Owner; nor do they think fit they ought to give such outward expressions of Love, by such uselesse actions, when as htey have a high esteem of their Suters Love, a perfect belief of their Merit, and a constant return of their affection, and a resolution to dye, or suffer any misery for their sakes if need required; besides, true Lovers have ever the Idea of their beloved in their Thoughts, by which they cannot forget their Memory, indeed Love-letters they may read often, because Letters are an injoyment of their discourse, although their persons be at a distance, and are also a recreation and delight in their Wits, if there be any Wit therein, but to kisse the Paper, they neither find pleasure, delight, non profit, neither to themselves, nor to their Beloved; the truth is, not one Writer amongst a thousand make Lovers woo either wisely, wittily, nobly, eloquently, or naturally; but either foolishly, meanly, unmanly, unhandsomely, or amorously, which is corruptly.

MATRON
Lady, you say very true, and some Romantical Writers, make long and tedious Orations, or long and tedious and fruitless discourse, in such times as requires sudden action.

LADY SPEAKER
You say right, as to speak when they are to fight; but for my part I hate to read Romances, or some Scenes in Plays, whose ground or Foundation is Amorous Love.

MATRON
When you read such Books, you must never consider the Subject that the Writer writes on, but consider the Wit, Language, Fancy, or Description.

SECOND MATRON
Most Reverend Sister, I suppose few read Romances, or the like Books, but for the Wit, Fancy, Judgement, and lively Descriptions; for they do not read such Books, as they do read Chronicles, wherein is only to be considered the true Relation of the History.

LADY SPEAKER
Most Grave and Wise Matronesse, I believe though none read Romances, or such like Books, whose ground is feigned Love, and Lovers, as they read Chronicles, whose ground should be unfeigned Truth; yet certainly, few read Romances or the like Books, either for the Wit, Fancy, Judgement or Descriptions, but to feed their Amorous Humours on their Amorous Discourses, and to rune their Voice to their Amorous Strains of Amorous Love; for it is to be observed, that those Books that are most Amorously penned, are most often read.

[Exeunt.

SCENE THE LAST

Enter the **ACADEMICAL GENTLEMEN**; to them enters a **SERVANT**.

MAN SERVANT
May it please your Worships, there is an Antient Gentlewoman that desires to speak with your Worships.

FIRST GENTLEMAN
I lay my life it is one of the Matrons of the Academy.

SECOND GENTLEMAN
Faith if the Humble Bee is flown out, the rest of the Bees will follow.

THIRD GENTLEMEN
I fear if they do, they will swarm about our Ears.

FOURTH GENTLEMEN
Yes, and sting us with their Tongues.

FIFTH GENTLEMEN
Let us send for her in.

SIXTH GENTLEMEN
I will go and Usher her in.

[He goes out.

[Enters with the **MATRON**; All the **GENTLEMEN** pull off their Hats.

MATRON
Gentlemen, the Ladies of the Academy have sent me unto you to know the Reason or Cause that you will not let them rest in quiet, or suffer them to live in peace, but disturb them in both, by a confused noise of Trumpets, which you uncivilly and discourteously blow at their Grate and Gates.

FIRST GENTLEMAN
The cause is, that they will not permit us to come into their Company, but have barricadoed their Gats against us, and have incloystred themselves from us; besides, it is a dangerous example for all the rest of their Sex; for if all women should take a toy in their heads to incloyster themselves, there would be none left out to breed on.

MATRON
Surely it is very fit and proper that young Virgins should live a retired life, both for their Education and Reputation.

SECOND GENTLEMAN
As for their Education, it is but to learn to talk, and women can do that without teaching, for on my Conscience, a woman was the first inventer of Speech; and as for their Retirement, Nature did never make them for that purpose, but to associate themselves with men: and since men are the chief Head of

their kind, it were a sign they had but very little Brain, if they would suffer the youngest and fairest women to incloyster themselves.

MATRON
Gentlemen pray give me leave to inform you, for I perceive you are in great Error of mistake, for these Ladies have not vowed Virginity, or are they incloystred; for an Academy is not a Cloyster, but a School, wherein are taught how to be good Wives when they are married.

THIRD GENTLEMEN
But no man can come to woo them to be Wives.

MATRON
No, but if they can win their Parents, or those thy are left in trust with, and get their good liking and consent, the young Ladies have learn'd so much Duty and Obedience, as to obey to what they shall think fit.

FOURTH GENTLEMEN
But we desire the Ladies good liking, we care not for their Friends; for the approvment and good liking of their Friends, without the Love of the Ladies, will not make us happy, for there is no satisfaction in a secondary Love, as to be beloved for anothers sake, and not for their own.

MATRON
If you be Worthy Gentlemen, as I believe you all are, their Love will be due to your Merits, and your Merits will perswade them to love you.

ALL THE GENTLEMEN
Well, if you will be our Mediator, we will surcease our Clamour, otherwise we will increase our noise.

MATRON

If you can get leave of their Parents, and Friends, I will endeavour to serve you, and shall be proud of the imployment that you shall be pleased to impose to my trust and management.

GENTLEMEN
And we shall be your Servants, for your favours.

[They all go out, with the **GENTLEMEN** waiting on her, with their Hats in their hands, Scraping and Congying to her.

MARGARET CAVENDISH – A CONCISE BIBLIOGRAPHY

Philosophical Fancies (1653)
Poems and Fancies (1653)
Philosophical and Physical Opinions (1655)
Nature's Pictures drawn by Fancie's Pencil to the Life (1656)
The World's Olio (1655)

Playes, (1662) folio, containing twenty-one plays including
Loves Adventures
The Several Wits
Youths Glory, and Deaths Banquet
The Lady Contemplation
Wits Cabal
The Unnatural Tragedy
The Public Wooing
The Matrimonial Trouble
Nature's Three Daughters (Beauty, Love and Wit) Part I & Part II
The Religious
The Comical Hash
Bell in Campo
A Comedy of the Apocryphal Ladies
The Female Academy
Plays never before printed (1668), containing five plays.
The Sociable Companions, or the Female Wits
The Presence
The Bridals
The Convent of Pleasure
A Piece of a Play
Orations of Divers Sorts (1662)
Philosophical Letters, or Modest Reflections upon some Opinions in Natural Philosophy maintained by several learned authors of the age (1664)
CCXI Sociable Letters (1664)
Observations upon Experimental Philosophy & Description of a New World (1666)
The Blazing World (1666)
The Life of William Cavendish, Duke, Marquis, and Earl of Newcastle, Earl of Ogle, Viscount Mansfield, and Baron of Bolsover, of Ogle, Bothal, and Hepple, &c. (1667)
Grounds of Natural Philosophy (1668)